CLASSI
Piano Solos for Kids

Arranged & Edited by
Robert Schultz

PREFACE

CLASSICAL Piano Solos for Kids includes 45 of the world's most beautiful and well-known melodies. The themes are drawn from ballets, operas, symphonies, choral music and chamber music of 32 of the great composers. This collection, as all others within the *Piano Solos for Kids Series*, is intended to serve as a repertoire and reading supplement for beginning and early grade piano students.

Teachers, students and parents will find within these pages a body of familiar, appropriate and reliable music, carefully and expertly crafted into stimulating solo arrangements suitable for beginners, first-year students and second-year students. The arrangements are written in either a five-finger format—melodies divided between the hands—or in very simple arrangements for both hands. Fingerings have been included, but sparingly. Tempo indications are in English. Special care has been taken to ensure that the student will encounter an accurate and consistent approach to editorial marks, providing a path to a clear understanding and reinforcement of the meaning of these important symbols of the music language.

Editor: *Robert Schultz*
Project Manager: *Tony Esposito*
Production Coordinator: *Zoby Perez*
Book Design & Illustration: *Jorge Paredes*

CONTENTS

CONTENTS

Title	Composer	Page No.

The Composers
Included in This Edition

The Baroque Period (1600-1750)

Tomaso Albinoni ....June 8, 1671–January 17, 1750

Johann Sebastian Bach ....March 21, 1685–July 28, 1750

Christoph Willibald Glück ....July 2, 1714–November 15, 1787

Jean Joseph Mouret ....April 16, 1682–December 22, 1738

Johann Pachelbel ....August ?, 1653–March 6/7, 1706

The Classical Period (1750-1830)

Ludwig van Beethoven ....December 15/16, 1770–March 26, 1827

Franz Joseph Haydn ....March 31, 1732–May 31, 1809

Wolfgang Amadeus Mozart..January 27, 1756–December 5, 1791

Gioacchino Rossini ....February 29, 1792–November 13, 1868

Franz Schubert ....January 31, 1797–November 19, 1828

The Romantic Period (1830-1900)

Georges Bizet..October 25, 1838–June 3, 1875

Alexander Borodin ....November 12, 1833–February 27, 1887

Johannes Brahms ....May 7, 1833–April 3, 1897

Max Bruch ....January 6, 1838–October 2, 1920

Paul Dukas ....October 1, 1865–May 17, 1935

Antonín Dvořák ....September 8, 1841–May 1, 1904

Edward Elgar..June 2, 1857–February 23, 1934

Gabriel Fauré..May 12, 1845–November 4, 1924

Umberto Giordano..August 27, 1867–November 12, 1948

Victor Herbert ....February 1, 1859–May 26, 1924

Engelbert Humperdinck ....September 1, 1854–September 27, 1921

Franz Lehar ....April 30, 1870–October 24, 1948

Pietro Mascagni..December 7, 1863–August 2, 1945

Felix Mendelssohn ....February 3, 1809–November 4, 1847

Jacques Offenbach ....June 20, 1819–October 4, 1880

Giacomo Puccini ....December 22, 1858–November 29, 1924

Bedrich Smetana..March 2, 1824–May 12, 1884

Peter Ilyich Tchaikovsky..May 7, 1840–November 6, 1893

Giuseppe Verdi ....October 10, 1813–January 27, 1901

Richard Wagner..May 22, 1813–February 13, 1883

The Twentieth Century (1900-2000)

Sergei Rachmaninoff...April 1, 1873–March 28, 1943

Igor Stravinsky ....June 17, 1882–April 6, 1971

Theme from
SYMPHONY No. 94
("Surprise Symphony")

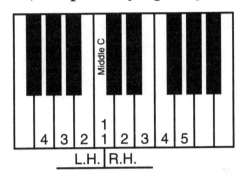

FRANZ JOSEPH HAYDN
Arranged by ROBERT SCHULTZ

Moderately

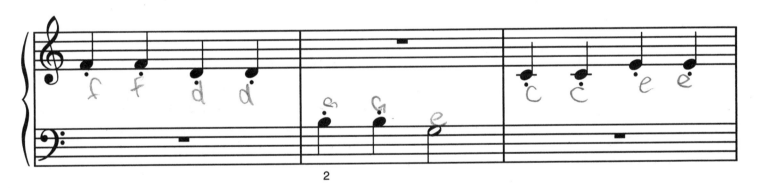

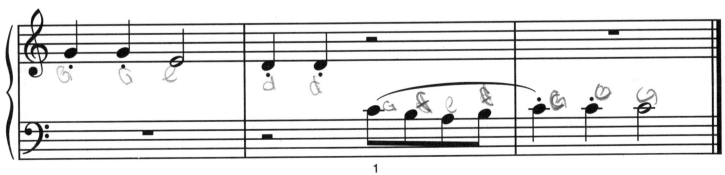

Theme from
THE MERRY WIDOW
(Waltz)

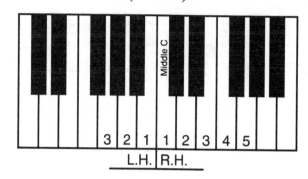

FRANZ LEHAR
Arranged by ROBERT SCHULTZ

Moderate waltz

Theme from The Merry Widow - 2 - 1

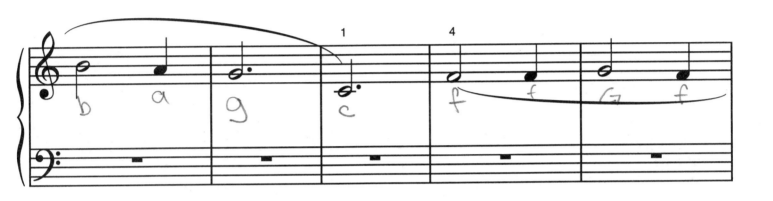

Theme from
PAVANE

GABRIEL FAURÉ
Arranged by ROBERT SCHULTZ

Moderately fast

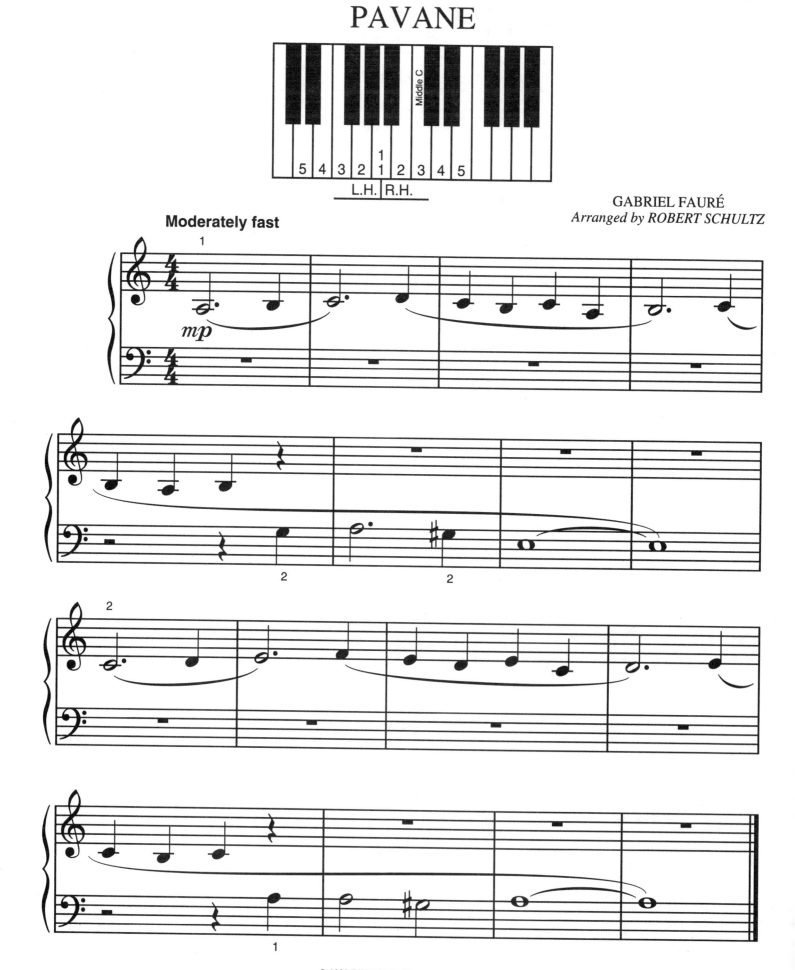

Theme from
WILLIAM TELL OVERTURE

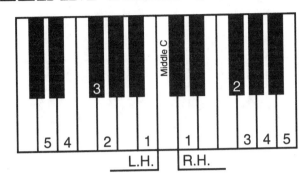

GIOACCHINO ROSSINI
Arranged by ROBERT SCHULTZ

Theme from
LA CI DAREM LA MANO
(from the opera *Don Giovanni*)

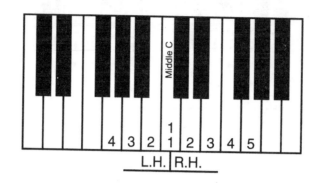

WOLFGANG AMADEUS MOZART
Arranged by ROBERT SCHULTZ

Moderately

Theme from La Ci Darem La Mano - 2 - 1

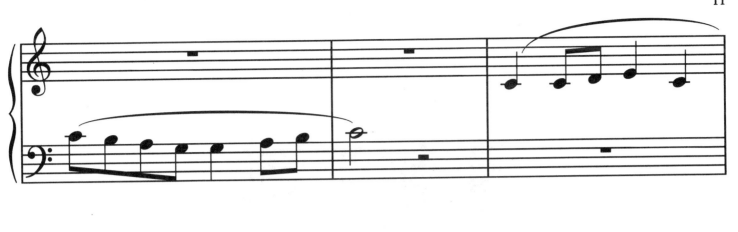

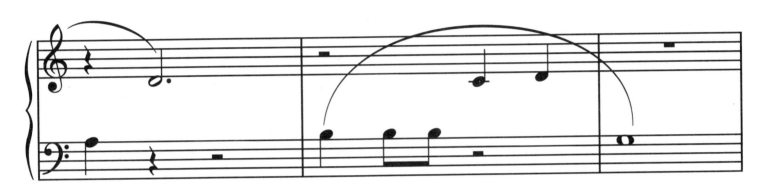

Theme from La Ci Darem La Mano - 2 - 2

Theme from
SYMPHONY No. 1

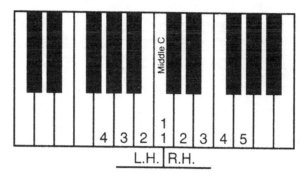

JOHANNES BRAHMS
Arranged by ROBERT SCHULTZ

Moderately

Theme from
SYMPHONY No. 9
("Choral Symphony")

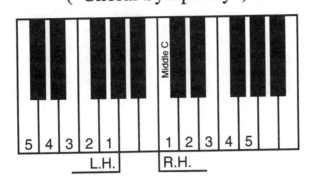

LUDWIG VAN BEETHOVEN
Arranged by ROBERT SCHULTZ

Moderately fast

Theme from
EVENING PRAYER
(from the opera *Hansel and Gretel*)

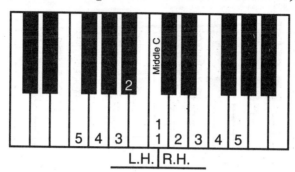

ENGLEBERT HUMPERDINCK
Arranged by ROBERT SCHULTZ

Slowly

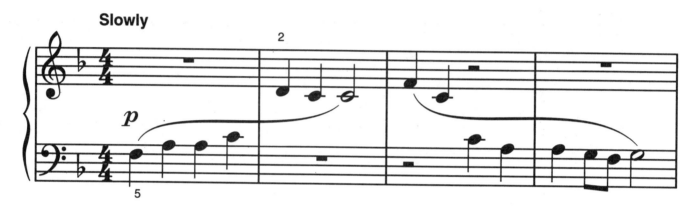

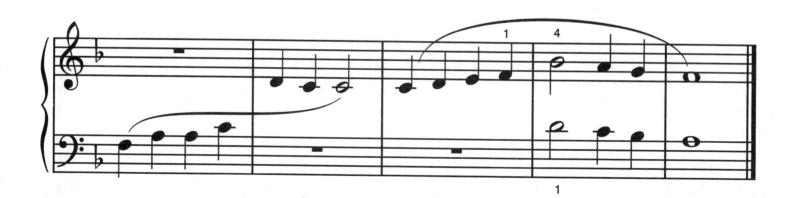

Theme from
BARCAROLLE
(from the opera *The Tales of Hoffmann*)

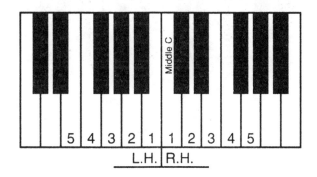

JACQUES OFFENBACH
Arranged by ROBERT SCHULTZ

Gently

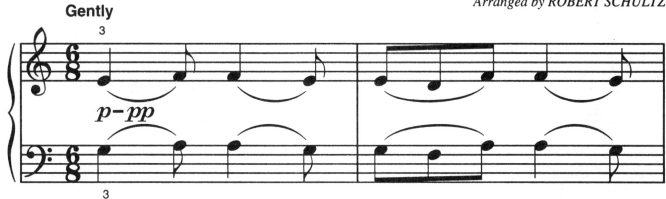

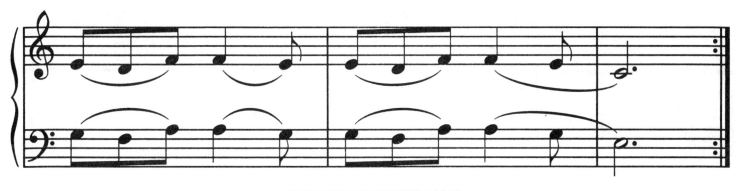

Theme from
POMP AND CIRCUMSTANCE

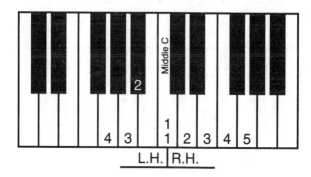

EDWARD ELGAR
Arranged by ROBERT SCHULTZ

Slow and majestic

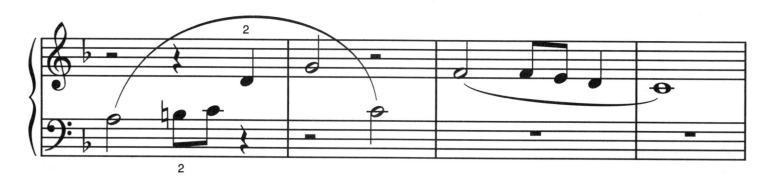

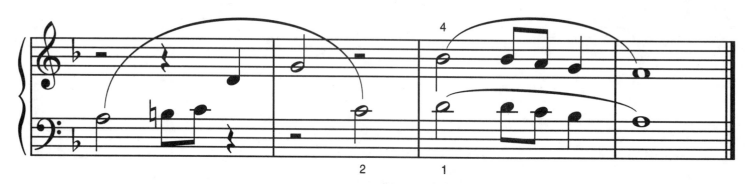

Theme from
POLOVETSIAN DANCE
(from the opera *Prince Igor*)

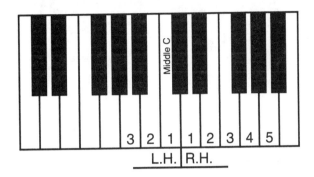

ALEXANDER BORODIN
Arranged by ROBERT SCHULTZ

Moderately fast

CRADLE SONG
(Wiegenlied)

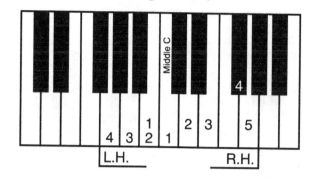

JOHANNES BRAHMS
Arranged by ROBERT SCHULTZ

Theme from
LA MAMMA MORTA
(from the opera *Andrea Chénier*)

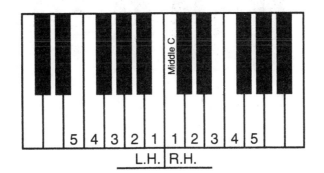

UMBERTO GIORDANO
Arranged by ROBERT SCHULTZ

Moderately

Theme from
LIBERA ME
(from the *Requiem*)

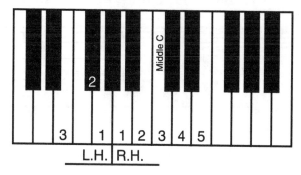

GABRIEL FAURÉ
Arranged by ROBERT SCHULTZ

Very moderately

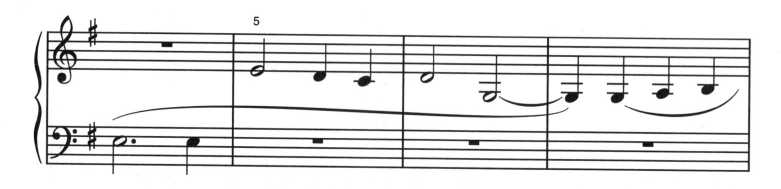

Theme from Libera Me - 2 - 1

Theme from
KOL NIDREI

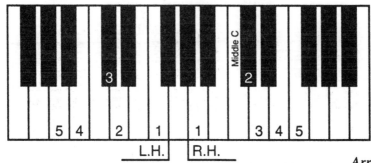

MAX BRUCH
Arranged by ROBERT SCHULTZ

Moderately slow

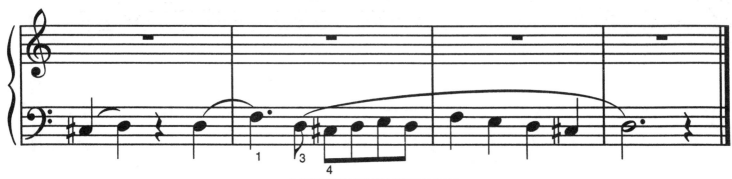

Theme from
SYMPHONY No. 9
("Great C Major Symphony")

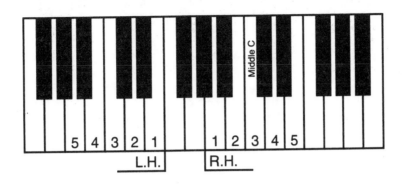

FRANZ SCHUBERT
Arranged by ROBERT SCHULTZ

Theme from
THE ANVIL CHORUS
(from the opera *Il Trovatore*)

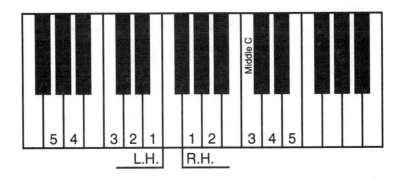

GIUSEPPE VERDI
Arranged by ROBERT SCHULTZ

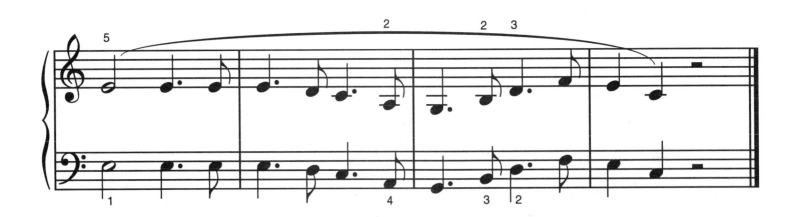

Theme from
SYMPHONY No. 5
(Movement III - *Waltz*)

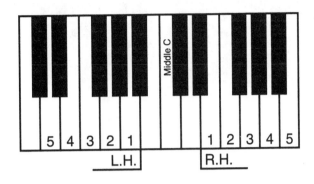

PETER ILYICH TCHAIKOVSKY
Arranged by ROBERT SCHULTZ

Waltz tempo

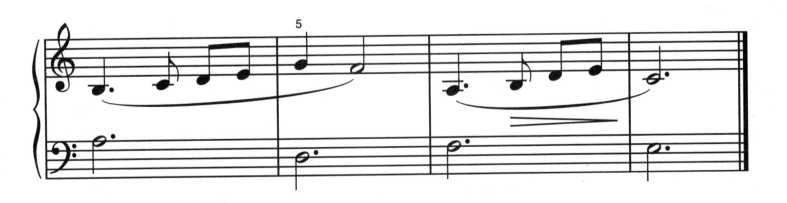

RONDEAU THEME
(from *Symphonic Suite No. 1*)

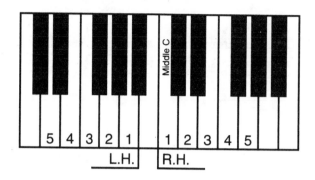

JEAN JOSEPH MOURET
Arranged by ROBERT SCHULTZ

Majestically

Rondeau Theme - 2 - 1

Rondeau Theme - 2 - 2

Theme from
THE SORCERER'S APPRENTICE

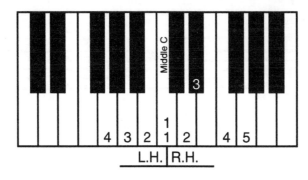

PAUL DUKAS
Arranged by ROBERT SCHULTZ

Quickly, mischievously

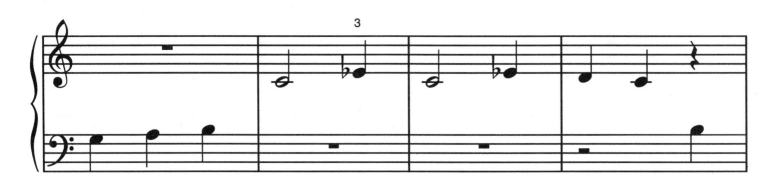

Theme from The Sorcerer's Apprentice - 2 - 1

Theme from The Sorcerer's Apprentice - 2 - 2

Theme from
MARCH OF THE TOREADORS
(from the opera *Carmen*)

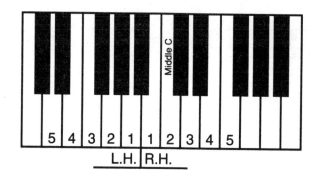

GEORGES BIZET
Arranged by ROBERT SCHULTZ

Bright march

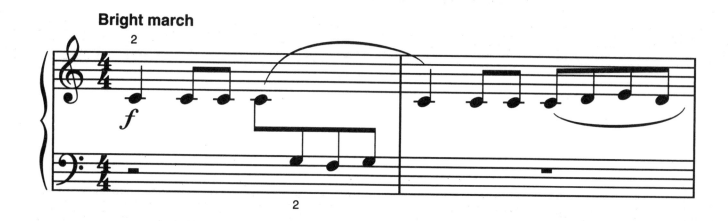

Theme from March of the Toreadors - 2 - 1

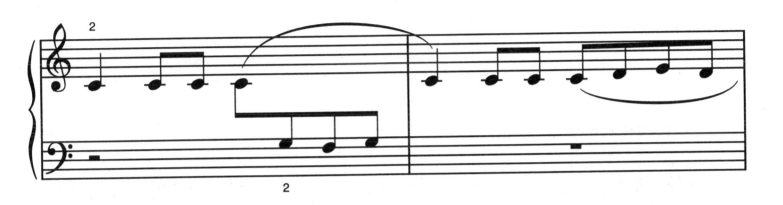

Theme from March of the Toreadors - 2 - 2

Theme from
WALTZ
(from the ballet *The Sleeping Beauty*)

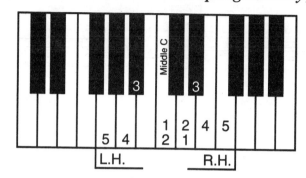

PETER ILYICH TCHAIKOVSKY
Arranged by ROBERT SCHULTZ

Waltz tempo

Theme from Waltz - 2 - 1

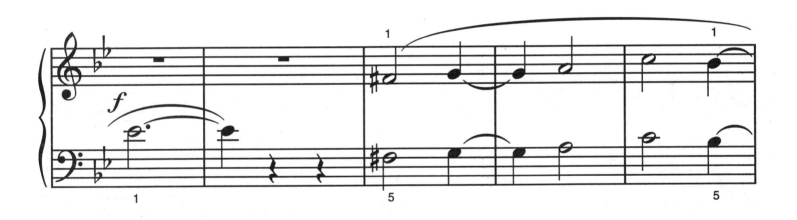

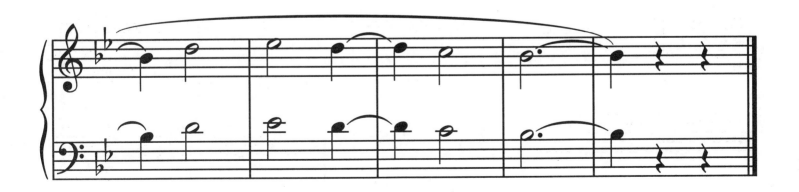

Theme from Waltz - 2 - 2

Theme from
VOCALISE

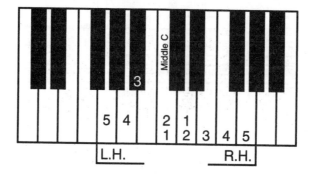

SERGEI RACHMANINOFF
Arranged by ROBERT SCHULTZ

Moderately slow

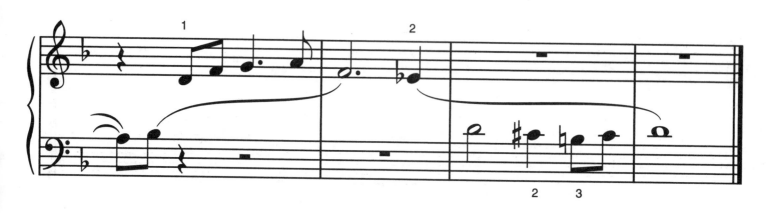

Theme from
UN BEL DI
(from the opera *Madama Butterfly*)

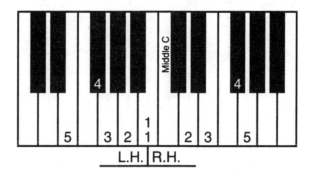

GIACOMO PUCCINI
Arranged by ROBERT SCHULTZ

Moderately slow

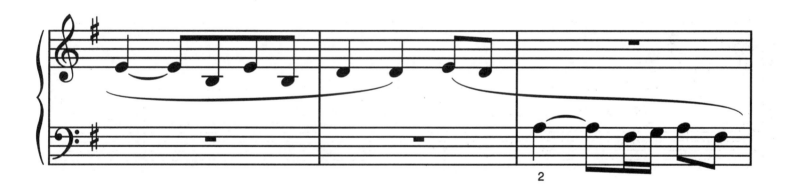

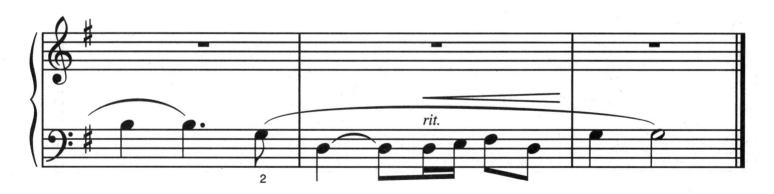

Theme from
RUSSIAN DANCE
(from the ballet *Petrushka*)

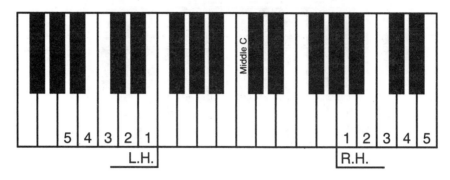

IGOR STRAVINSKY
Arranged by ROBERT SCHULTZ

Fast and crisp

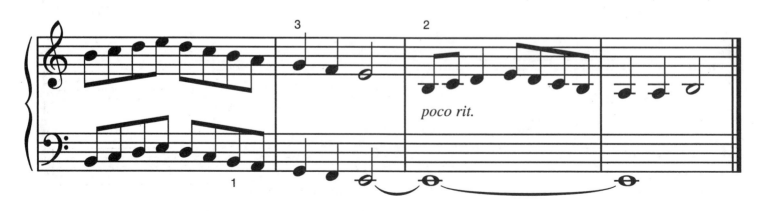

Theme from
CAN-CAN
(from the operetta *La Vie Parisienne*)

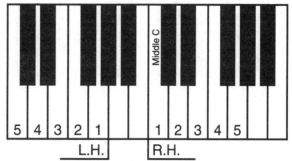

JACQUES OFFENBACH
Arranged by ROBERT SCHULTZ

Theme from
TOYLAND
(from the operetta *Babes In Toyland*)

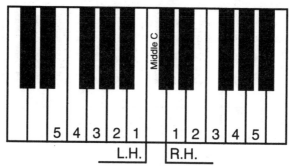

Music by
VICTOR HERBERT
Arranged by ROBERT SCHULTZ

Dreamily

Theme from
JESU, JOY OF MAN'S DESIRING
(from Cantata No. 147)

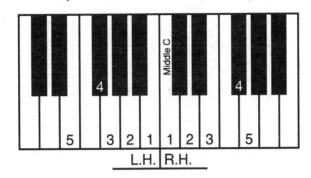

JOHANN SEBASTIAN BACH
Arranged by ROBERT SCHULTZ

Very flowing

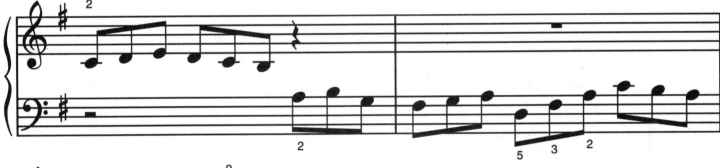

Theme from
CHE FARÒ SENZA EURIDICE?
(from the opera *Orfeo ed Euridice*)

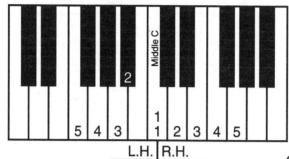

CHRISTOPH WILLIBALD GLÜCK
Arranged by ROBERT SCHULTZ

Moderately

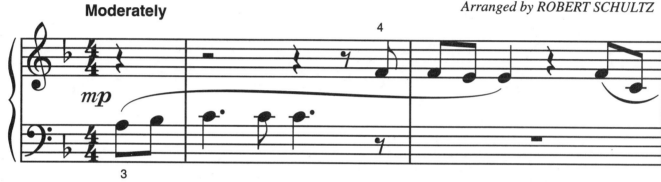

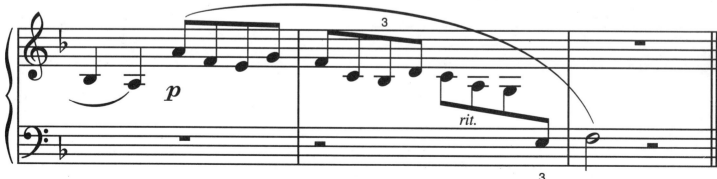

Theme from
BRIDAL CHORUS
(Wedding March from *Lohengrin*)

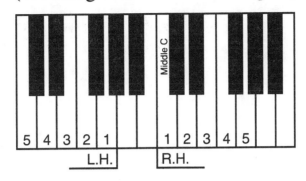

RICHARD WAGNER
Arranged by ROBERT SCHULTZ

Theme from
THE WEDDING MARCH
(from the opera *A Midsummer Night's Dream*)

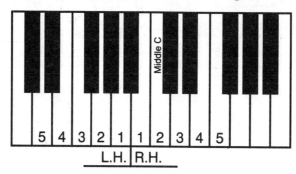

FELIX MENDELSSOHN
Arranged by ROBERT SCHULTZ

Majestically

Theme from
VIOLIN CONCERTO

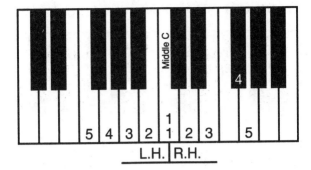

FELIX MENDELSSOHN
Arranged by ROBERT SCHULTZ

Moderately fast

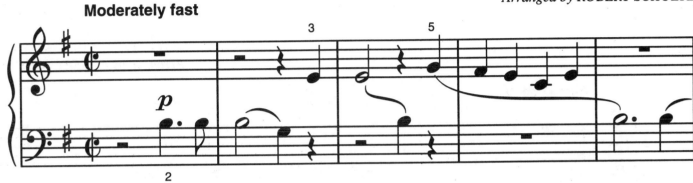

p

crescendo

f

Theme from
SWAN LAKE
(Finale from the ballet *Swan Lake*)

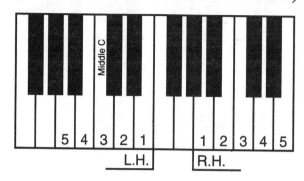

PETER ILYICH TCHAIKOVSKY
Arranged by ROBERT SCHULTZ

Theme from
SLAVONIC DANCE

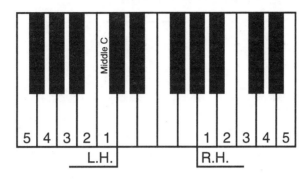

ANTONÍN DVOŘÁK
Op. 46, No. 7
Arranged by ROBERT SCHULTZ

Moderately fast

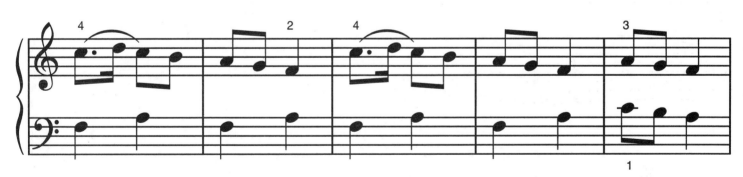

Theme from
TOREADOR SONG
(from the opera *Carmen*)

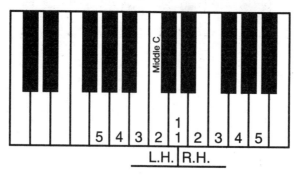

GEORGES BIZET
Arranged by ROBERT SCHULTZ

With spirit

Theme from
ADAGIO

TOMASO ALBINONI
Arranged by ROBERT SCHULTZ

O MIO BABBINO CARO
(from the opera *Gianni Schicchi*)

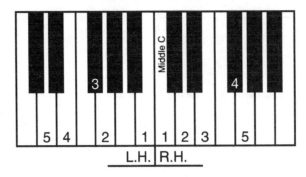

GIACOMO PUCCINI
Arranged by ROBERT SCHULTZ

Moderately

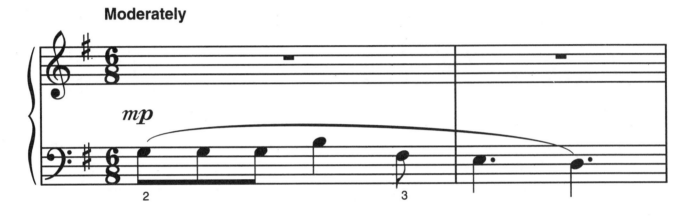

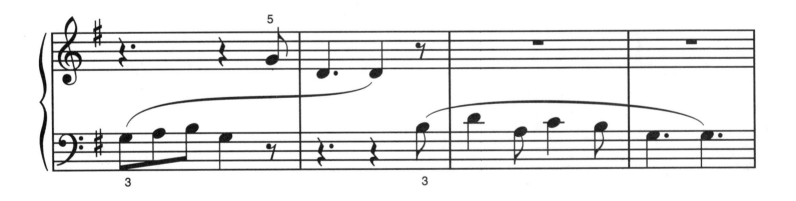

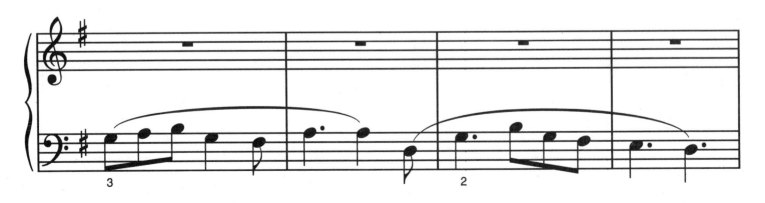

O Mio Babbino Caro - 2 - 1

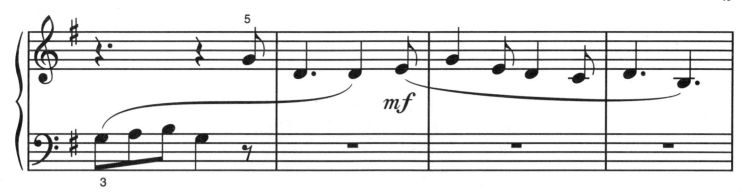

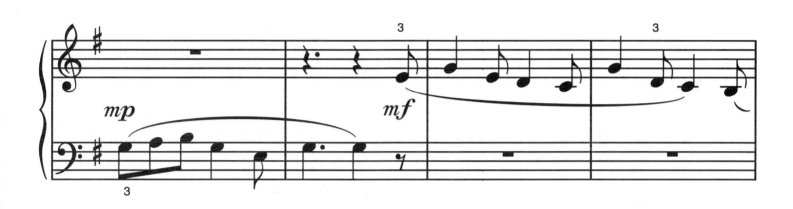

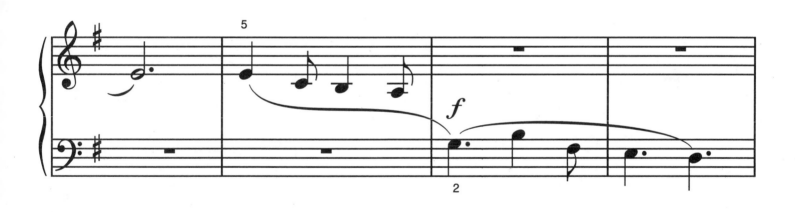

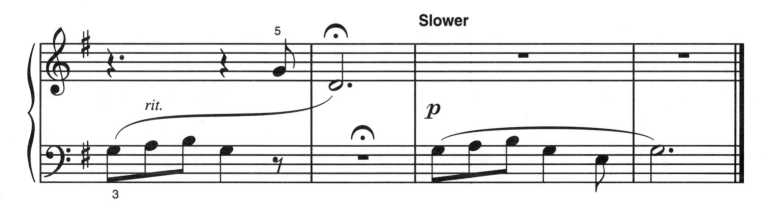

O Mio Babbino Caro - 2 - 2

Theme from
LARGO
(from *The New World Symphony*)

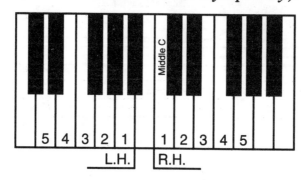

ANTONÍN DVOŘÁK
Arranged by ROBERT SCHULTZ

Slowly

Theme from Largo - 2 - 1

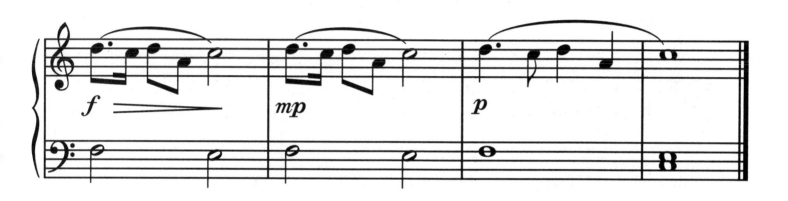

Theme from
SYMPHONY No. 40

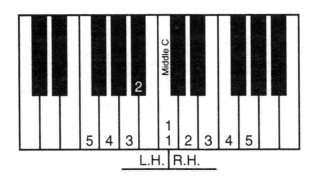

WOLFGANG AMADEUS MOZART
Arranged by ROBERT SCHULTZ

Fast

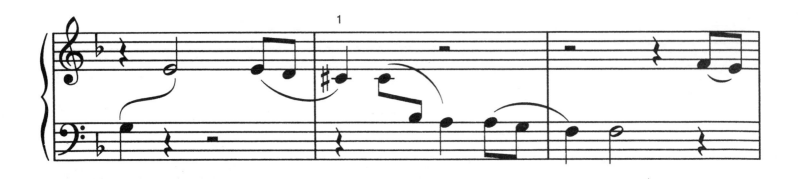

Theme from Symphony No. 40 - 2 - 1

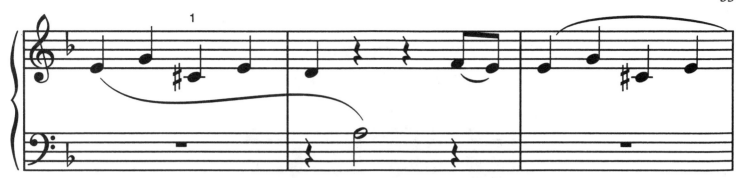

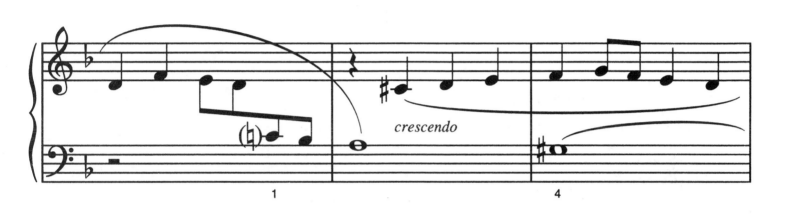

crescendo

f

1. 2.

diminuendo

p

Theme from Symphony No. 40 - 2 - 2

Theme from
SYMPHONY No. 8
(*Unfinished*)

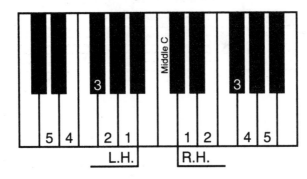

FRANZ SCHUBERT
Arranged by ROBERT SCHULTZ

Moderately fast

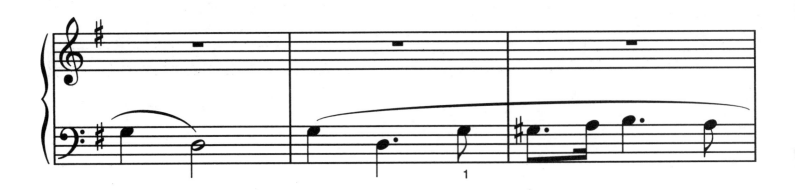

Theme from Symphony No. 8 - 2 - 1

Theme from
INTERMEZZO
(from the opera *Cavalleria Rusticana*)

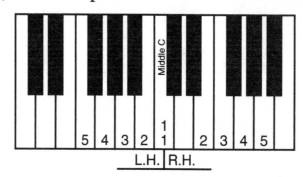

PIETRO MASCAGNI
Arranged by ROBERT SCHULTZ

Moderately

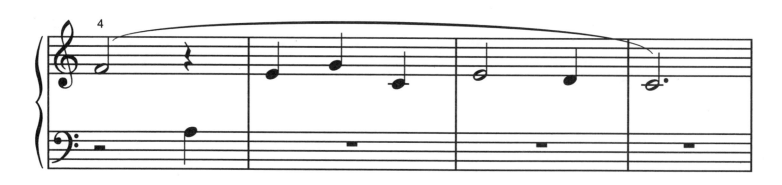

Theme from Intermezzo - 2 - 1

Theme from Intermezzo - 2 - 2

Theme from
THE MOLDAU
(Vltava)
(from the Symphonic Poem Cycle *My Country*)

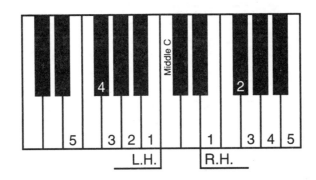

BEDŘICH SMETANA
Arranged by ROBERT SCHULTZ

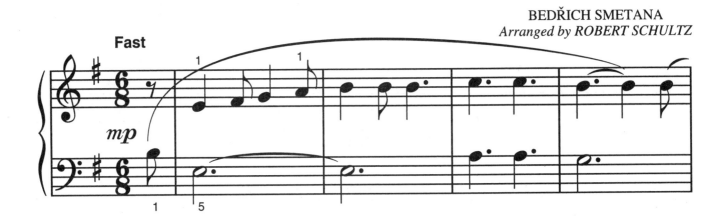

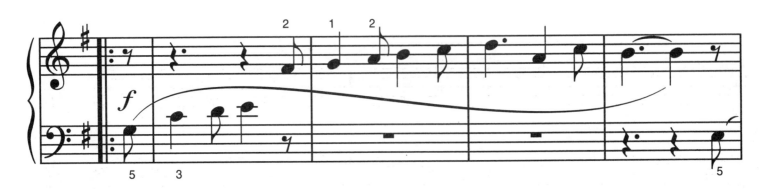

Theme from The Moldau - 2 - 1

Theme from
DANCE OF THE SUGAR PLUM FAIRY
(from *The Nutcracker Suite*)

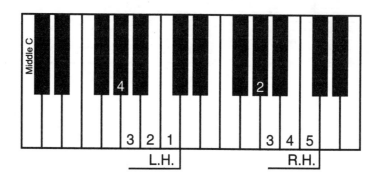

PETER ILYICH TCHAIKOVSKY
Arranged by ROBERT SCHULTZ

Moderately, delicately

both hands 8va

Theme from Dance of the Sugar Plum Fairy - 2 - 1

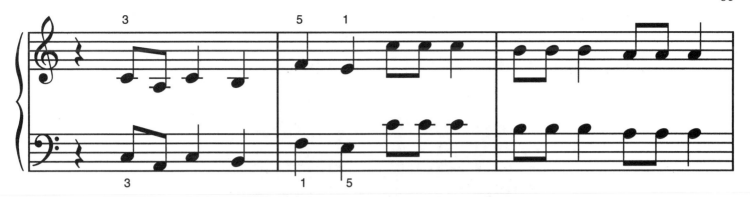

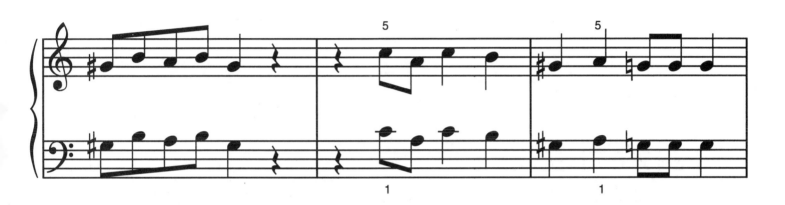

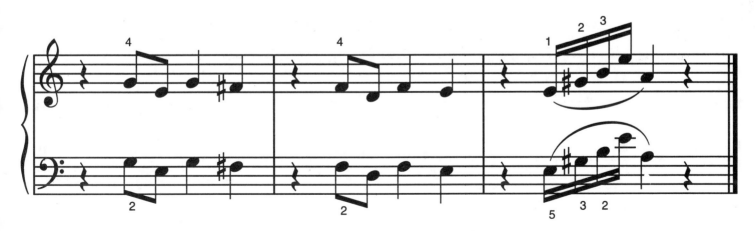

Theme from Dance of the Sugar Plum Fairy - 2 - 2

Theme from
RUSSIAN DANCE
(from *The Nutcracker Suite*)

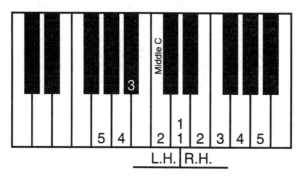

PETER ILYICH TCHAIKOVSKY
Arranged by ROBERT SCHULTZ

Fast and lively

Theme from
CANON IN D

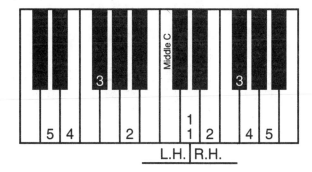

JOHANN PACHELBEL
Arranged by ROBERT SCHULTZ

CLASSICAL MUSIC COLLECTIONS
from the Schultz Piano Library
by Robert Schultz

Superb editions of the world's best-loved classical music
for piano students at every level from beginner to late intermediate.

Classical Collections for beginning piano students:

An introduction to classical music through 5-finger arrangements of well-known themes and beautiful melodies from operas, symphonies, ballets, chamber music and vocal works.

Classical Piano Solos for Kids (AF9823)
45 pieces, 64 pages, Preface, Composer list - names/dates/period.

Fun with 5 Finger Classical Themes (AF9765)
35 pieces, 48 pages, Preface.

Performance Plus Series: Classical Themes, Book 1 (AF9638)
10 pieces with teacher accompaniments, 24 pages.

Classical Collections for early–late intermediate piano students:

Classical Piano Solos for Young Adults (AF9551)
Early intermediate - 10 easy pieces in their original form by various composers, plus 20 arrangements of well-known themes from the symphony and opera; 48 pages, Preface.

Performance Plus Series: Classical Themes, Book 2 (AF9644)
Early intermediate - 11 arrangements with teacher accompaniments of themes from symphonies and the opera; 24 pages.

100 Best Loved Piano Solos - Teaching Pieces (AF9603)
Early intermediate - 75 easy piano solos in their original form by composers from all periods, plus 25 arrangements of opera, symphony, vocal and chamber music themes; 156 pages.

100 Best Loved Piano Solos - Composer Pieces (AF9503)
Late intermediate - 90 piano solos in their original form by composers from all periods, plus 10 arrangements of orchestral, vocal and chamber masterpieces; 256 pages.

**Available at leading music dealers everywhere,
from Warner Bros. Publications**

AD 369